Dr. Hossain Al Mamun, Touhida Sultana

Camus' Meursault in "The Outsider" Archetype of an Absurd Man

A Critical Study

Document Nr. V212190

Dr. Hossain Al Mamun, Touhida Sultana

Camus' Meursault in "The Outsider" Archetype of an Absurd Man

A Critical Study

GRIN Verlag

Die Deutsche Bibliothek verzeichnet diese Publikation in der Deutschen Nationalbibliografie; detaillierte bibliografische Daten sind im Internet über http://dnb.d-nb.de/ abrufbar.

1. Auflage 2011
Copyright © 2011 GRIN Verlag GmbH
http://www.grin.com
Druck und Bindung: Books on Demand GmbH, Norderstedt Germany
ISBN 978-3-656-40575-7

Camus' Meursault in *The Outsider*: Archetype of an Absurd Man

Dr. Hossain Al Mamun* and Touhida Sultana**

Abstract: This paper explores Meursault's brusque mannerisms that lead to society judging him and ultimately hating him, as he is judged to be a threat. Meursault did not care about anything or anybody, but himself, and his own little pleasures and the necessities of the moment. He has no feelings, does not care to "advance" his life in the same way that others expect. It demonstrates how Meursault is a rebel in the eyes of society by his actions and upholds him as the archetype of an absurd man.

Key words: Archetype, Absurd, Camus, Meursault

In the essay "Camus' The Outsider," Jean-Paul Sartre explains that Camus' book is more of an 'experience of the absurd' for readers than a 'novel' because it uses literary approaches to identify and clarify the absurdity of life. The absurd is both a 'state of fact' and what people obtain from this 'state of fact'. He is also the man who does not hesitate to draw the inevitable conclusions from a fundamental absurdity. He is not only a person without a drive but also a person who is content with anything. Meursault is the perfect example of an absurd man.

*Associate Professor, Department of English, Shahjalal University of Science & Technology, Sylhet and ** MA in English, Department of English, Shahjalal University of Science & Technology, Sylhet, Bangladesh

1

His attitude towards life has been one of listless detachment; throughout the text, he never says more than he feels and refuses to conform to the norms of his society. He lives for the moment: at work, in his relationship with Marie, in his choice of friends such as Emmanuel, Raymond and Salamano, in his lack of remorse for the murder and finally in his attitude towards the chaplain and Christianity, in lacking the need for forgiveness.

Meursault resists being typecast into an archetypal moral category in many of his deeds and actions. Many of his actions in Part One of the novel help contribute to the fuzzy picture of the character. For example, Meursault starts off at the beginning of the story by showing how absurd he is. He does not seem to care about anything in his life nor does he know anything about his own mother. He had sent her to a home so that she could be taken care of, which he saw as a burden. Throughout the first chapter of the book, he asked for several days of in order to go to his mother's funeral: "Maman died today. Or yesterday maybe, I don't know. I got a telegram from the home: "Mother deceased. Funeral tomorrow. Faithfully yours." That doesn't mean anything. Maybe it

was yesterday." (Camus 9). This conveys that Meursault is very insensitive because no "ordinary" person would ever say that especially after his mother's death. A person should be a little sensitive when in situations like it. Meursault is not concerned with the feelings or emotions of others around him. At his mother's funeral, Meursault does not regret his mother's death and instead of mourning he takes the wake as insignificant that he borrows a black tie and armband for the funeral. He is not willing to spend money when he would use them only one time. Almost misses his bus for the funeral. Actually he faces life and death with the same easy indifference. That's why his mom's death is meaningless to him: it's all the same to him. On the way to the funeral, during the vigil and the funeral itself, his reactions are mostly physical, when he enters the mortuary; his attention is not in the wooden box. He notices the skylight above and the bright clean-whitewashed walls. Even after the mortuary keeper has left, his attention is not on the coffin, he reacts to the sun, and getting low and the whole room was flooded with a pleasant, mellow light. He denies seeing the body of his mom. Indeed he smokes a cigarette and drinks white

coffee before the unviewed body. According to him she is dead but he is alive, is sweaty and hot and doing what he is expected to do for a funeral. His mom gave him birth, brought him up. Now he becomes adult. And as become adult, he and his mom were no longer close. In Meursault's words: "They had nothing else to say each other" (Camus 20). And at this moment in his life, he can't yield to the rituals of frantic, emotional breast-beating because of his mother's death. During the funeral procession Meursault is not concerned with his mom's existence in an after life. He is not torn by religious agony or a sense of loss. During the long hours of funeral, he isn't in mourning. Rather he is uncomfortable and embarrassed. He thinks that he is wasting the day and he has to tolerate the lengthy and boring ordeal. His mom's friend Thomas Perez points out that Meursault has no sympathy for it. His only thoughts are focused on getting back to Algiers and going to bed for twelve hours: "the blood red earth spilling over Maman's casket, more people, voices of the village, waiting in front of the café", the instant drone of the motor, and my joy when the bus entered Algiers and I knew I was going to bed and sleep for twelve

hours." (Camus 22). Even after the day of funeral when he wakes up he realizes how exhausting the funeral was. He thinks to go to swimming, as we find no feelings about his mother. By a chance on the beach he meets a girl who worked for a short time in his office. They go to watch a comedy movie. He befriends Marie and goes on living as if nothing has happened. Even that night they go to his home to have sex.

In the beginning of chapter three, Meursault's boss asks him how old Maman was and Meursault answers "About sixty, so as not to make a mistake..." (Camus 29). This scene was a bit awkward because it is not usual for a person to not care for his parents. He smoked, thought of the beach, and talked of Saturdays spent with Marie, but seldom thought about anything else. His mother died, but all he could think of was the two hour ride to the old people's home in Marengo. It is too strange. Meursualt continues to show us how indifferent he is. He has no real thoughts, no real care about anything he does in life.

Even when he meets Marie, he still does not know how to love her or what love even means. He does not understand the

whole concept of having choices and deciding which one's he wants: "Marie came around for me and asked me if I wanted to marry her. I said it didn't make any difference to me and that we could if she wanted to."(Camus 44) but all Meursault could think of was sex. This shows that Meursault is blunt; he has no regard for the feelings and or concerns for others. In this connection Camus said that Meursault was a "Poor and naked man." As he hide nothing. As the story slowly progress, Meursault also moves forward towards what the meaning of his life is. When Meursault takes Marie to the beach with Raymond, we start to see a glimpse of want in Meursault. He started observing another couple on the beach, which made him want to have a relationship like theirs. "For the first time maybe, I really thought I was going to get married... Together again, Marie and I swam out ways, and we felt a closeness as we moved in unison and were happy."(Camus 52) For the first time, he started to show that wanted and was looking forward to something different, to a relationship that will change his life. He is slowly removing the indifference that feels about his life. Thus Camus presents him as the existentialist in the first part,

a man bored with life, a man with little feelings for anything or anybody, except sex, cigarettes, and the beach, all physical aspects of life.

While Meursault is walking at the beach finds the Arab that Raymond had had a confrontation with earlier. With no apparent reason, Meursault pulls out a gun and shoots five shots at the Arab, killing him instantly. In that moment, he knew that this was going to be the start of a change in his life: "I fired four more times at the motionless body... And it was like knocking four quick times on the door of unhappiness."(Camus 60) he is then put into prison and a court trial is on its way to convict him. In the second half, he is presented more philosophically, more deeply, as the prisoner condemned to his cell, stripped of all his beloved physical desires and replaced with memories and emotions, things that He was missing in the first part of the novel. At first, he does not seem very happy about being in jail. But for the first time has accepted that his home is now the jail: "I felt that I was at a home in my cell and that my life was coming to a standstill there."(Camus 71) He is able to sit there and just think about his actions. He realizes that his

whole life is about to change and there's no way out. Everything is real to him now and he knows he cannot escape the truth. His cell is his home. There is no more running away and no more dreaming for something that he cannot have. All he has now is to accept the reality and the consequences that go along with his actions. He continues to move to a new state of mind. He thinks and reflects a lot more on what has happened in his life. He was judged on something completely different, his unique personality of not caring about the society's customs and practices. He is a candid person who will do things that he wants, and will not lie to make his life easier. A refusal to lie is not usual, and his unusual behavior resulted in a sort of breaking of social conventions and made everyone around him feel uncomfortable, threatened and fearful.

Through Meursault's life experience, Albert Camus tried to reveal that our society is often prejudiced against people who are different. And although lying is thought to be morally incorrect; in reality, society often does want us to lie. This is why the jury judged him for not having feelings for his mother and not because he had killed a man. He was judged for who he was and was hated

by society. Thus he was seen as a menace to society. The small things like the death of his mother and how he turned down Marie's proposal that didn't really seem to have a major role in the beginning of the story, turned out to have such a great impact on the whole story. By the time of the actual trial, he already knew that he was going to tried guilty and be sentenced to death. Everyone will die eventually and what matters more is how much your life meant rather than how many years you were allowed to live. He realizes that we all are born, we all die, and we all will eventually be forgotten. Only at this point is He able to achieve happiness. He knows death is unavoidable and that he has no choice. He is has to able to just accept death: "for the first time, in that night alive with signs and stars, I opened myself to the gentle indifference of the world." He realizes that nothing lasts forever and death is just putting an end to life. There shouldn't be anything scary about death because it's going to happen. What you can do is accept it and leave earth happily. Now his thoughts shift away from the murder itself to his attitudes and beliefs. He is able to break through his indifference and make sense out of his life. When he

becomes aware that his life will end soon, that is when he truly understands the meaning of life. So in the second half of The Stranger, Camus depicts society's attempt to manufacture meaning behind Meursault's actions. The trial is absurd in that the judge, prosecutors, lawyers and jury try to find meaning where none is to be found.

For Camus, life has no rational meaning or order. We have trouble dealing with this notion and continually struggle to find rational structure and meaning in our lives. This struggle to find meaning where none exists is what Camus calls, the absurd. Camus wrote *The Outsider* as an enticement to his readers, to think about their own mortality and the meaning of their existence. The hero or anti-hero of *The Outsider* is Meursault. His life and attitudes possess no rational order. His actions are strange to us, there seems to be no reason behind them. We are given no reason why not he chooses to marry Marie or gun down an Arab. For this, he is a stranger amongst us. And when confronted with the absurdity of the stranger's life society reacts by imposing meaning on the stranger. Camus does not want us to think of Meursault as 'the

stranger who lives 'outside' of his society' but of a man who is 'the stranger within his society'. So, He was not an outsider; he was a member of his society–a society that wants meaning behind action. Camus wrote *The Outsider* in the early 1940's. Both stories centered around the WWII atmosphere and the change and realization that came with this environment. Throughout Camus' novel the concepts of the struggle for freedom, the obstacle of choices, the responsibility of citizens in hard times, and the essence of human nature are constantly referenced to through Camus' unique writing style.

In the novel the author tried to show the world of an absurd man, Meursault, who's life mattered little, a rebel who himself was bored with life. In *The Outsider*, he lives a life free from society's constraints. Throughout the novel, he is either unaware or indifferent to the customs and expectations of society. He does not care to "advance" his life in the same way that others expect, such as through marriage and job promotion. Instead, he concludes that one life is as good as another. It is this quotation that defines his philosophy of life as well as the belief that ultimately sets him

"free." He defines the value of his life, so he does not wish to gain the respect or admiration of others. In this way, he is able to do what he truly wants to and not what other people expect him to. Through the eyes of an ordinary person, he is a menace to society because of his philosophy towards life. His emotions and thoughts cannot be compared to other people. Society has created rules so binding that any person breaking them is comdemned as an alien, an outsider. For Meursault it is an insult to his reason and a betrayal of his hopes; for Camus it is the absurdity of life.

Thus, Camus creates a mythology of the absurd. Camus wrote, "Meursault, for me, is a poor and naked man in love with the sun which leaves no shadows. He is far from being totally deprived of sensitivity for he is animated by a passion, profound because it is tacit, the passion for the absolute and for truth. It is still a negative truth of living and feeling, but a truth without which no conquest of the self or of the world is possible."(Camus 119) ... "Meursault is the man who answers but never asks a question, and all his answers so alarm a society which cannot bear to look at the truth." Camus successfully described Meursault as a brutally

truthful person with those quotes. Meursault's brutal truth and honesty rubbed some people the wrong way, and it led to his undoing.

Works Cited:

Camus, Albert, *The Outsider.* Trans. Joseph Laredo. Penguin Books, London, England, 1982.

Carey, Gary. *Cliff's Notes on 'Camus' The Stranger'.* Lincoln. Nebraska, 1979.

Keegan, Diana. "Meursault the Stranger – Absurd Hero *Par Excellence*". Web. 7 June 2011.

Rogers, Pat. *An outline of English Literature.* 2nd Ed. New York: Oxford UP, 1998.

Schwerner, Armand. *Monarch Notes: 'Albert Camus's The Stranger.'* New York, 1970.